STEM *trailblazer* BIOS

THEORETICAL PHYSICIST
BRIAN GREENE

MATT DOEDEN

Lerner Publications
Minneapolis

The publisher wishes to thank Brian Greene for providing some of the photos that appear in this book.

The author thanks Patrick Schelling of the University of Central Florida for his help in grasping the physics described in this book.

Lerner Publications Company
A division of Lerner Publishing Group, Inc.
241 First Avenue North
Minneapolis, MN 55401 USA

For reading levels and more information, look up this title at www.lernerbooks.com.

Content Consultant: Claudia Frugiuele, PhD, Postdoctoral Associate, Theoretical Physics, Fermilab

Library of Congress Cataloging-in-Publication Data

Doeden, Matt, author.
    Theoretical physicist Brian Greene / by Matt Doeden.
        pages   cm. — (STEM trailblazer bios)
    Includes index.
    ISBN 978–1–4677–5790–4 (lib. bdg. : alk. paper)
    ISBN 978–1–4677–6279–3 (eBook)
    1. Greene, B. (Brian), 1963-—Juvenile literature. 2. Physicists—United States—Biography—
Juvenile literature. I. Title. II. Series: STEM trailblazer bios.
    QC16.G636D64 2015
    530.092—dc23   2014015916

Manufactured in the United States of America
1 – PC – 12/31/14

The images in this book are used with the permission of: © iStockphoto.com/Frank Vandenbergh, p. 4; © Thos Robinson/Getty Images, pp. 5, 21, 23, 25; Courtesy of Brian Greene, pp. 6, 9; © Steve Dunwell/Photolibrary/Getty Images, p. 7; NASA/JPL-Caltech/STScI, p. 10; © Evan Otto/Science Source, p. 11; © Designua/Dreamstime.com, p. 12; © Laguna Design/Science Source, p. 14; © Silvia Otte/CORBIS, p. 16; © Todd Strand/Independent Picture Service, p. 18; © Lynn Goldsmith/CORBIS, p. 19; New Line Cinema/Courtesy Everett Collection, p. 20; © Lynn Goldsmith/CORBIS, p. 24; © Robert Voets/CBS /Getty Images, p. 26; AP Photo/PBS/NOVA and Pixeldust Studios, p. 27.

Front cover: © Frederick M. Brown/Getty Images.

Main body text set in Adrianna Regular 13/22. Typeface provided by Chank.

CONTENTS

Brian grew up in Manhattan. It is one of five boroughs, or sections, that form New York City.

NEW
PERSPECTIVES

Brian Greene has always loved math. He was born on February 9, 1963, in New York City, New York. By the age of five, he was practicing multiplication for fun. But young Brian wasn't content with multiplying small numbers. He would tape pieces of paper together so that he could multiply thirty-digit numbers!

Brian's father, Alan Greene, was a musician. Alan had dropped out of high school as a teenager. But he understood that his son was gifted, and he wanted to help nurture that gift. Alan taught his son to view the world in different ways. He invented games to engage Brian's imagination.

In one game, they would observe everyday events and imagine them from wild perspectives. For example, if they saw

Brian has spent his life learning about how the universe works.

a coin drop to the sidewalk, Brian might describe the scene as if he were an ant on top of the coin, falling to the sidewalk. It was a simple and fun game. But it also taught Brian to think creatively.

QUEST FOR KNOWLEDGE

Brian learned to question everything around him. When he was nine, his mother served a meal of ribs. Brian was horrified to see the meat hanging off the bones. For the first time, he really connected the meat to the animal it had come from. Brian decided that he'd never eat meat again. He's been a vegetarian ever since.

By sixth grade, Brian's math teacher had nothing left to teach him. So he suggested Brian go to nearby Columbia University to find a tutor. Brian went from office to office in search of a tutor. He finally found one in graduate student Neil Bellinson. Bellinson introduced Brian to more advanced mathematics. Brian soaked up every bit of it.

From an early age, Brian was interested in mathematics.

HIGHER EDUCATION

Greene graduated from Stuyvesant High School in 1980. From there, he went on to Harvard University in Cambridge, Massachusetts. Greene still had a passion for math. But a new interest had also captured his attention—physics. Physics is the study of how matter and energy interact. Scientists

At Harvard University, Greene learned that his love of math could be turned into a career in physics.

TECH TALK

"Science is a full-body experience. It makes the heart beat fast when a result is working well. I've long . . . felt [that] the public has a misconception about science: that it's something that only makes use of the mind. But it really touches the soul when you reveal deep truths about the universe."

—*Brian Greene*

use physics to try to explain how the universe works. For Greene, physics offered a new way to understand the world around him.

Four years later, Greene graduated from Harvard as a Rhodes scholar. This meant that he'd been recognized as one of the most gifted students in the world. As a Rhodes scholar, he earned a scholarship to attend Oxford University in England. His focus there remained on physics. But Greene didn't limit himself. He also took up acting with a theater group. Acting helped him become more comfortable speaking in front of large groups. He would use this skill later in life.

Greene took acting classes while attending Oxford University. The classes increased his comfort with public speaking.

Chapter 2

Physicists explore matters such as how our universe began and how it may change in years to come.

BIG IDEAS

The goal of physics is to explain how the universe works. Greene learned that the universe seems to exist as two separate realms. In the first realm, everything we can see and touch follows the same set of rules. These rules apply to everything from giant stars to tiny specks of dust. The study of these rules is often called **classical physics**.

But at the scale of a single **atom** or smaller, a second realm exists. Particles in this realm follow a different set of rules. The study of these rules is called **quantum physics**. This type of physics became a focus of Greene's studies at Oxford.

Scientists have known about the quantum realm for more than one hundred years. It's a mysterious place where particles behave in ways that seem impossible. They can vanish from one place only to reappear in another. The more scientists

The atom is so tiny that it can be observed only with a powerful microscope. Quantum physics studies particles that are the size of an atom or smaller.

know about a particle, the less they seem to know about how it will behave. All this uncertainty makes the quantum realm a strange place with many unanswered questions.

THE THEORY OF EVERYTHING

One day while Greene was walking through the halls of Oxford, a poster caught his attention. The university was hosting a lecture on **string theory**—or "the theory of everything," as the poster put it. This relatively new theory was supposed to explain more about the quantum realm.

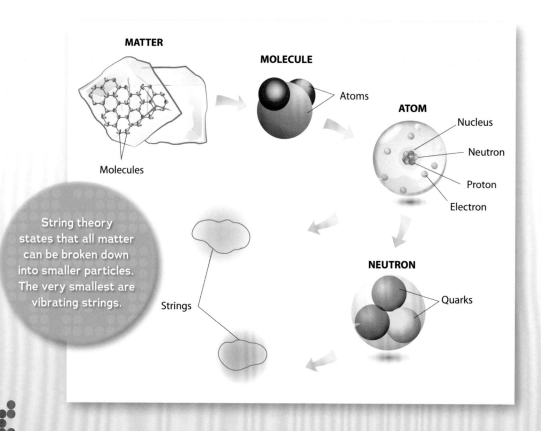

MATTER

Molecules

MOLECULE

Atoms

ATOM

Nucleus

Neutron

Proton

Electron

String theory states that all matter can be broken down into smaller particles. The very smallest are vibrating strings.

Strings

NEUTRON

Quarks

Greene was interested. So he went to the lecture. What he heard there changed the direction of his life. String theory became his biggest focus. Greene set up a study group with friends after the lecture. Their goal was to learn as much about string theory as they could.

Greene learned that string theory is as wild as the quantum realm it tries to explain. The main idea is that inside every particle of matter there are tiny vibrating strings of energy. This would mean that every object around us is a collection of these tiny vibrating strings. But these strings could not exist in the three-dimensional world that we see. Instead, the math behind the theory suggests that more **dimensions** of space must exist. And not just one or two more. There may be as many as ten or eleven! We just can't see them.

FOCUSING ON STRINGS

String theory can be confusing. But it made sense to Greene. String theory attempts to bring together the different laws of physics into one combined theory. If string theory is proven true, it will have a huge impact on how we understand the universe. This possibility excited Greene.

Greene earned his doctorate degree from Oxford in 1986. He then returned to Harvard to continue his research.

At Harvard, Greene helped make several major discoveries. These included one called mirror symmetry. Greene showed that the dimensions of space that we can't see might be curled up into different shapes. He was able to find two shapes that looked different but had the same physics. This discovery has helped mathematicians make predictions. It has also helped scientists further their ideas about how string theory might work.

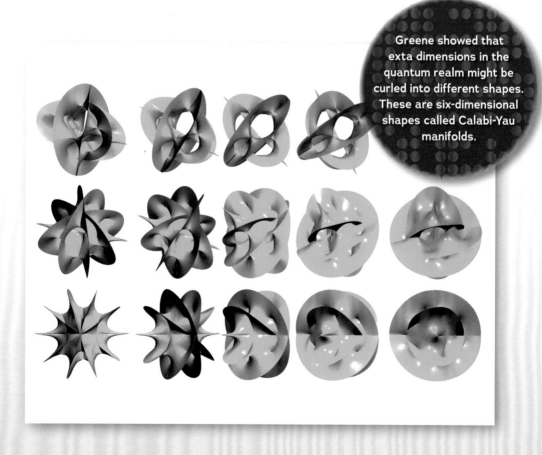

Greene showed that exta dimensions in the quantum realm might be curled into different shapes. These are six-dimensional shapes called Calabi-Yau manifolds.

TECH TALK

"Physicists often use the term *elegant* to describe a solution to a problem that is as powerful as it is simple. It's a solution which cuts to the heart of an important problem with such clarity that it almost leaves no doubt that the solution is either right or at least on the right track. And string theory is just that kind of solution."

—*Brian Greene*

In 1990, Greene accepted a teaching job at Cornell University in Ithaca, New York. His ability to communicate complex ideas in simple language made him a natural teacher. In 1996, he moved back to New York City to teach at Columbia University.

Greene had become one of the leading physicists on string theory. Yet few people outside the scientific community knew who he was. That was about to change.

Chapter 3

Greene began teaching in the 1990s. His passion for teaching continues today.

A BROADER AUDIENCE

String theory quickly became well known within the physics community. But the science behind the theory was very complex. This made it difficult for the general public to understand. Most people didn't get how string theory worked and why it was an exciting idea.

Greene found beauty in what he called the elegance of string theory. It was thrilling for him to peel back layers of the universe and discover how it might work. Greene loved to teach, but he wanted to reach a larger audience. He wanted to share string theory with everyone instead of just with fellow scientists.

By the late 1990s, he had a plan for exactly how to do that. Greene started writing his first book.

BRINGING SCIENCE OUT OF THE CLASSROOM

Greene has always had a passion for teaching science. And not just in a college classroom. Greene is famous for offering lectures that are open to anyone. In 2014, he took things to a new level. Greene started his own online classroom at worldscienceu.com. Anyone can take the exciting courses he teaches on classical physics, quantum physics, and much more!

THE ELEGANT UNIVERSE

Greene's book came out in 1999. He titled it *The Elegant Universe: Superstrings, Hidden Dimensions, and the Quest for the Ultimate Theory.* The book was a major achievement. It does something that many people had thought impossible. It explains string theory in a way that nonscientists can understand. In the book, Greene uses real-world analogies to help people understand the quantum universe.

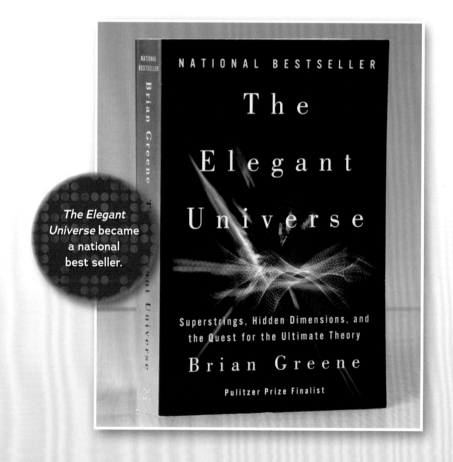

The Elegant Universe became a national best seller.

NATIONAL BESTSELLER

The Elegant Universe

Superstrings, Hidden Dimensions, and the Quest for the Ultimate Theory

Brian Greene

Pulitzer Prize Finalist

Greene presents ideas from *The Elegant Universe* at the 2006 Aspen Ideas Festival.

The book soared up best-seller lists and sold more than a million copies. It was nominated for several awards including the Pulitzer Prize. Suddenly, people wanted to know who Brian Greene was. Reporters wanted interviews. Greene was even featured on TV talk shows such as *Nightline* and *Late Night with Conan O'Brien*.

Greene thrived in front of the camera. Audiences were attracted to the joy he expressed while talking about science. Some compared him to Carl Sagan, a scientist who became famous for his ability to bring science to the masses.

Greene was in demand. In 2000, he served as a science consultant for the feature film *Frequency*. Greene even appeared in the film as himself!

Frequency is a science ficton thriller starring Jim Caviezel *(below)* and Dennis Quaid.

SCIENCE ON THE SCREEN

It didn't stop there. In 2003, Greene helped the television series *NOVA* turn his book into a three-hour documentary. Greene narrated the program. It received rave reviews.

A year later, Greene published his second book. It was titled *The Fabric of the Cosmos: Space, Time, and the Texture of Reality.* The book challenges much of what we think we know

TECH TALK

"Sometimes there can be a tension between wanting something to be more entertaining yet having to be well aware of what that might be doing to the accuracy of the science. For me [working on the *NOVA* documentary] was constantly keeping a watch out to make sure that the science ultimately was dictating what we could and couldn't do."

—*Brian Greene*

about space and time. Once again, Greene promoted his book with a media tour. One of the highlights was an appearance on the *Late Show with David Letterman*. Greene tackled topics ranging from string theory to time travel. Near the end, Letterman joked, "Does your head ache all the time?"

Greene's career was really taking off. And so was his personal life. He married television journalist and producer Tracy Day. In 2005, the couple welcomed a son named Alec.

Greene attends the 2008 World Science Festival with his wife, Tracy.

In 2011, Greene published a new book. It is called *The Hidden Reality: Parallel Universes and the Deep Laws of the Cosmos*. The book explains the idea that there might be more than one universe. It was another smash hit. A reviewer from the *New York Times* wrote, "If extraterrestrials landed tomorrow and demanded to know what the human mind is capable of accomplishing, we could do worse than to hand them a copy of this book."

Greene also returned to television in 2011. He teamed up with *NOVA* for a four-part series called *The Fabric of the Cosmos*. And he even got a chance to dust off his acting skills for a guest appearance on the popular sitcom *The Big Bang Theory*.

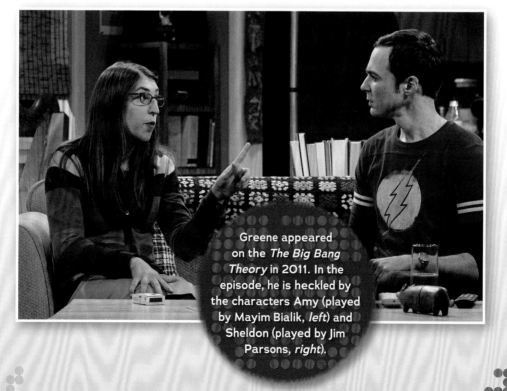

Greene appeared on the *The Big Bang Theory* in 2011. In the episode, he is heckled by the characters Amy (played by Mayim Bialik, *left*) and Sheldon (played by Jim Parsons, *right*).

Greene hosted the miniseries *NOVA: The Fabric of the Cosmos* in 2011.

STICKING WITH SCIENCE

Greene has become a pop culture star. But he's never stopped being a scientist. He continues to research string theory. One of his goals is to explain why our universe appears to have only three dimensions. The math behind his work is very complex. But one possibility that Greene has considered is the black hole electron. Electrons are the building blocks of every atom. And Greene thinks it's possible that electrons might really be tiny black holes!

Will Greene ever prove it? Will scientists ever be able to prove that tiny vibrating strings make up everything in the universe? Maybe not. But that won't stop Greene from trying to solve some of the universe's greatest mysteries. And if he succeeds, he'll be sure to explain it to us in a way that we can all understand.

TECH TALK

"The universe is rich and exciting, and there's stuff that can knock you over every day if you're privy to it. . . . The more we can translate [it] into a familiar language, the more rich and exciting it is for everybody."

—*Brian Greene*

TIMELINE

1963
Greene is born February 9 in New York City.

1970
String theory is born, based on the work of several physicists.

1984
Greene graduates from Harvard University. He goes on to Oxford as a Rhodes scholar.

1990
Greene is part of a team that proves the possibility of mirror symmetry. Later that year, he accepts a teaching position at Cornell University in Ithaca.

1996
Greene accepts a teaching position at Columbia University in New York City.

1999
Greene publishes his first book, *The Elegant Universe: Superstrings, Hidden Dimensions, and the Quest for the Ultimate Theory*. It is a huge success.

2003
Greene helps create and narrate the documentary film based on his book.

2008
Greene and his wife, Tracy Day, found the annual World Science Festival in New York City.

2011
Greene publishes *The Hidden Reality: Parallel Universes and the Deep Laws of the Cosmos*. He also works on a new PBS documentary, *The Fabric of the Cosmos*.

2014
Greene helps to launch the World Science U website.

SOURCE NOTES

8 J. R. Minkel, "The String Is the Thing: Brian Greene Unravels the Fabric of the Universe," *Columbia Magazine*, Spring 2006, accessed April 15, 2014, http://www.columbia.edu/cu/alumni/Magazine/Spring2006/green.html.

15 Brian Greene, "Brian Greene, Author of *The Elegant Universe*," interview by Patricia Schwarz, *The Official String Theory Web Site*, accessed April 15, 2014, http://www.superstringtheory.com/people/bgreene.html.

22 Brian Greene, interview with *NOVA*, "A Conversation with Brian Greene," edited by Peter Tyson, *NOVA Online*, October 28, 2003, http://www.pbs.org/wgbh/nova/physics/conversation-with-brian-greene.html.

22 "Brian Greene on *David Letterman*," YouTube video, 9:00, on the *Late Show with David Letterman* on CBS on March 23, 2005, posted by "annas890's channel," January 3, 2010, https://www.youtube.com/watch?v=9P3iymn1yzc.

26 Timothy Ferris, "Expanding Horizons," *New York Times*, February 4, 2011, http://www.nytimes.com/2011/02/06/books/review/Ferris-t.html?_r=1.

28 Gregory Kirschling, "Master of the Universe," *Entertainment Weekly*, February 27, 2004, http://www.ew.com/ew/article/0,,592972,00.html.

GLOSSARY

atom
the smallest part of any element that can exist on its own

black hole
an invisible object in space that pulls everything into it, including light

classical physics
the study of things larger than an atom

dimensions
extensions in a given direction, such as length, width, or height

quantum physics
the study of the universe at scales smaller than an atom

string theory
the idea that all matter is made up of tiny vibrating strings of energy

FURTHER INFORMATION

BOOKS

Greene, Brian. *Icarus at the Edge of Time*. New York: Alfred A. Knopf, 2008. Read Greene's first book for kids—a retelling of the Icarus myth set in outer space!

Ventura, Marne. *Astrophysicist and Space Advocate Neil deGrasse Tyson*. Minneapolis: Lerner Publications, 2014. Discover another popular scientist with big ideas about the universe.

Zuchora-Walske, Christine. *We're the Center of the Universe! Science's Biggest Mistakes about Astronomy and Physics*. Minneapolis: Lerner Publications, 2015. Learn about scientific ideas from the past that turned out to be totally wrong!

WEBSITES

Brian Greene—Official Website
http://www.briangreene.org
Read more about Greene's career and watch clips of his TV appearances.

PBS.com—*The Elegant Universe*: Part 1
http://video.pbs.org/video/1512280538
Watch the first part of the documentary film based on Greene's popular book.

String Theory for Kids
http://stringtheory4kids.wordpress.com
Learn more about string theory and how it works.

Expand learning beyond the printed book. Download free, complementary educational resources for this book from our website, www.lerneresource.com.

INDEX

ABOUT THE AUTHOR

Matt Doeden studied journalism at Mankato State University, where he worked at the college newspaper for three years. Doeden went on to work as a sportswriter for the Mankato paper and then got a job as an editor for a children's book publisher. In 2003, Doeden decided to start his own business as a freelance writer and editor. Since then, he has written and edited hundreds of books on high-interest topics such as cars, sports, and airplanes, as well as curricular topics such as geography, science, and math.